The Best 50
DAIQUIRIS, MOJITOS

AND OTHER RUM DRINKS

Joe Wylde

BRISTOL PUBLISHING ENTERPRISES
Hayward, California

ISBN: 1-55867-287-7

Cover design: Frank J. Paredes
Cover photography: John A. Benson
Food stylist: Susan Broussard
Illustration: Caryn Leschen

THE ORIGINS OF RUM

Rum drinks have come a long way since Carmen Miranda boosted their popularity with the song – "Drinking rum and coca cola." Indeed, she may well have given the impression that "rum and coke" was all there was to the celebrated "Cuba Libre" – a drink which found much favor with such famous personalities as Ernest Hemingway and John F. Kennedy, just to mention two.

The word "rum" may be derived from the Malayan word "brum" or "bram". Rum is distilled mainly from cane sugar, and is produced in the West Indian Islands. Jamaica and Demerara are big producers of rum, but there are very fine rums originating in Trinidad, Barbados, Venezuela and Cuba.

The sugar cane plant is a tall perennial grass that is widely grown in warm regions. It is distinct from the root plant called sugar beet, which is also used for producing white sugar but which is not used for the production of rum. Sugar beet is grown in colder climates.

There are 2 kinds of Jamaican rum: "common" or "clean" rum, and "flavored" or "German" rum. The latter is used almost exclusively for blending with the lighter types of spirit.

Demerara rums are light in appearance, but are often very high in alcohol.

The deep brown color of some rums — such as Myers — is imparted by caramel or by storage in sherry casks, or by both.

Tafia is an inferior quality rum produced in Martinique and elsewhere in the Caribbean.

As a guide, rum cocktails are made from some variation of the following ingredients: $1\frac{1}{2}$ oz. rum, $\frac{1}{2}$ oz. lime juice, $\frac{1}{2}$ to $\frac{3}{4}$ oz. liqueur or fruit juice, and garnishes of various kinds to match or complement the ingredients.

THE STORY OF DAIQUIRIS

There is a small town on the east coast of Cuba called Daiquiri. The story goes that an American engineer called Cox worked there for some years but found the local rum a little fiery for his taste and decided to moderate it with lime. Thus the Daiquiri was born. Sometime further on, an American naval officer named Johnson met up with Cox at Daiquiri and was introduced to the potion by him. Johnson subsequently brought the drink to the attention of his friends at the Army and Navy Club in Washington, where it became so popular that a lounge is named after it.

There are skeptics who maintain that the Cubans were well acquainted with the Daiquiri in its various guises long before Cox and Johnson. Anyway, it's a nice story, and its truth or otherwise will not spoil the reader's enjoyment of this excellent cocktail.

NAMING THE MOJITO

The name Mojito (pronounced "moheeto") may well be a derivation of the name of the insect whose name is the same in English and Spanish – the mosquito. Perhaps "Stinger" might be a good translation but for the fact that the Mojito has no unpleasant after effects. On the contrary, a well-made Mojito can have a warm and soothing effect on a summer evening. One of the fringe benefits of drinking Mojitos is that the muddled mint ingredient tends to improve the flavor of one's breath.

MODIFIERS OR MIXERS

These are the additional ingredients in rum cocktails that blend with the rum base to create a new flavor. They may be distilled spirits, fortified wines, fruit juices, or carbonated water. Fresh juices work best in almost all cocktails, but you may find more variety in packaged juices. Lime or lemon juices are the favorite choices for rum cocktails, but orange may be called for on occasion.

ACCENTS

Accents are the final distinguishing touch in cocktails. Bitters, herbal liqueurs, peels and flowers are all used, singly, or in various combinations, to improve a drink's flavor or to enhance its appearance.

TWISTS

Cut twists from the peel of the citrus fruit. Twists contain all sorts of aromatic oils. When preparing twists, be sure to remove all traces of pith as this will make the drink bitter. Because of its larger size, a more elegant twist may be cut from a lemon than a lime. The twist should be about $1/4$ inch wide. When about to serve the drink, twist the peel over the glass so the oils may mix into the drink. Then hang the twist on the rim of the glass.

SQUEEZES, WHEELS AND WEDGES

For a lemon wheel or squeeze, cut a center slice from the lemon; put a small cut on the side and hang the squeeze on the rim of the glass. Your guest can then add the juice to his/her drink according to taste.

Prepare a lime squeeze or wedge by cutting the fruit lengthwise in quarters and then cutting the quarters crosswise This garnish is always used in the *Cuba Libre,* pages 37 and 38.

MARASCHINO CHERRIES

Maraschino cherries are cherries which have been soaked in a sugar syrup, flavored and dyed. Red maraschino cherries are usually almond-flavored, while green maraschinos are mint-flavored. They are popular in rum drinks, but never use more than 1 because their sweetness could overpower the essential flavor of the drink.

"MUDDLING" MINT

Mint has very hardy and resilient leaves. It is a universal favorite as a garnish, either floating on top or as an ingredient. In the case of the Mojito, muddled mint is one of the ingredients, and a floating sprig forms the garnish. To muddle mint, simply use a spoon or other utensil to carefully crush the leaves against the side of the glass, releasing the mint oil and aroma into the drink. If you do not take this step, the mint will still look — and be — fresh and unaffected when the drink is gone, and will have added little flavor to the recipe.

CORDIALS AND SYRUPS

Cordials and syrups are added to a drink to counter the sharp or tart taste imparted by the rum and lemon, lime or bitters used. Many commercially produced cordials and syrups are available, but it is both inexpensive, easy and handy to make your own *Simple Syrup* of sugar and water, as outlined on page 8.

SIMPLE SYRUP

This is an extremely useful sweetener, called for in many cocktails. It will keep in the refrigerator for long periods. When prepared, it is thick and very sweet. Use with caution to avoid oversweetening your drinks.

2 cups sugar
1 cup boiling water

Stir to dissolve sugar in boiling water. Cool and store in the refrigerator. Mixture should be very thick.

ESSENTIAL EQUIPMENT

For these who would like to make standard cocktails at home or to experiment with recipes of their own, here is a list of utensils necessary:

shaker
jigger
strainer
juicer
pint glass
barspoon
knife (small/sharp)
cutting board

dull knife or ice pick
scoop
muddler
crusher
corkscrew
bottle opener
garnishes

MEASURES AND MEASUREMENTS

In this book the measures in the recipes are usually given in metric measurements. Occasionally the recipes call for a teaspoon or a table-spoon measure. A dash means a very small amount, at the discretion of the pourer.

The jigger is the usual measure used by barmen. It is a small cup hold-ing 1½ ounces and is often double-ended with the smaller end giving exactly ½ a jigger, or ¾ ounce.

You may find a graduated shot glass or medicine glass easier to use and to obtain. The jigger, in fact, resembles an egg cup, which would make a useful standby for an emergency. If there is really nothing else available, remember that 1 tbs. = ½ ounce. and 3 tbs = 1 jigger.

BLUE BOY

Angostura bitters are named after the port town of Angostura, Venezuela. Bitters are made from a blend of tropical herbs, plants and spices, and are the single most widely distributed bar item in the world. As their name implies, they counteract the sweetness of many cocktail ingredients.

2 oz. dark rum
3/4 oz. sweet vermouth
1/2 oz. orange juice
1 dash angostura bitters
orange wheel for garnish

Shake all ingredients in a cocktail shaker over cracked ice. Strain into a chilled cocktail glass. Garnish with orange wheel.

APPLE PIE

There are lots of variations on this recipe — many include apple juice or apple brandy — but this version is a classic: clean and smooth. Try adding a little apple juice to taste if you prefer a sweeter drink.

1½ oz. dark rum
1 oz. sweet vermouth
½ oz. lime juice
1 dash grenadine
lemon wheel for garnish

Shake all ingredients in a cocktail shaker with cracked ice. Strain into a chilled cocktail glass. Garnish with a lemon wheel.

CAPTAIN'S BLOOD

In song and story, rum has always been loosely associated with pirates and sailing ships and wooden legs. There's even a popular brand of rum called "Captain Morgan's."

1½ oz. dark rum
½ oz. lemon juice
2 dashes angostura bitters

Shake all ingredients in a cocktail shaker over cracked ice. Strain into a chilled cocktail glass. Garnish with a lime squeeze.

CUBANO

Like most of the drinks in this book, this cocktail will taste much better when made with fresh juices. Fresh pineapple juice has a stronger flavor than packaged juice and cuts the flavor of the alcohol more effectively.

2 oz. dark rum
3/4 oz. lemon juice
1/4 oz. pineapple juice
lime twist or pineapple wheel for garnish

Shake all ingredients in a cocktail shaker with cracked ice. Strain into a chilled cocktail glass. Garnish with a lime twist or pineapple wheel.

THE ANNE SHERIDAN

This drink was named for the film star Anne Sheridan, the original "It Girl" of the fifties.

1½ oz. dark rum
¾ oz. curaçao
¾ oz. lime juice
lime wedges for garnish

Pour all ingredients into a glass and shake with cracked ice. Strain into a chilled cocktail glass. Garnish with a lime squeeze.

HOOVER

Among many great quotes, President Herbert Hoover famously defined the cocktail hour as, "the pause between the errors and trials of the day and the hopes of the night".

1½ oz. dark rum
1½ oz. sweet vermouth
1 dash curaçao
orange twist for garnish

Shake all ingredients in a cocktail shaker with cracked ice. Strain into a chilled cocktail glass. Garnish with an orange twist.

JAMAICA RUM

If you want to get in the groove for the rhumba, this should do the trick. Or, try making it with Woods 100-proof dark rum. If you do this, be careful: 100-proof alcohol is very strong stuff.

2 oz. dark rum
¾ oz. lime juice
1 tsp. *Simple Syrup,* page 8
lime squeeze for garnish

Shake all ingredients in a cocktail shaker with cracked ice. Strain into a chilled cocktail glass. Garnish with a lime squeeze.

MAI TAI #1

The name "Mai Tai" is Polynesian in origin and means "good" in Tahitian. One glass of this could make you feel like wearing a hula skirt. However, you might want to have a second Mai Tai before you decide. Almond syrup is a good substitute if you cannot find orgeat.

2½ oz. dark rum
½ oz. lemon juice, or ¾ oz. lime juice
½ oz. curaçao

1 splash grenadine
1 splash orgeat syrup
½ oz. dark rum
cherry for garnish

Shake rum, juice, curaçao, grenadine and orgeat in a cocktail shaker with cracked ice. Strain into a wine goblet or collins glass filled with ice. Top with dark rum. Garnish with a paper umbrella or a cherry and a flower blossom.

MAI TAI #2

One of the most well known rum cocktails, the Mai Tai was invented by "Trader Vic" Bergeron in 1944. This version adds apricot brandy.

3 oz. dark rum
1 oz. curaçao
1 oz. apricot brandy
juice of 1 lime
2 dashes orgeat syrup or almond syrup
2 dashes *Simple Syrup,* page 8
mint sprig for garnish

Into a cocktail shaker ²/₃ filled with ice, add dark rum, curaçao, apricot brandy, lime juice, orgeat syrup and simple syrup. Place ½ of lime hull in a chilled old-fashioned glass and top up with crushed ice. Shake and strain drink into glass. Garnish with a sprig of mint.

PIKAKI

Pikaki is an Hawaiian flower with a gorgeous fragrance somewhat similar to that of jasmine.

2 oz. dark rum
1/2 oz. orange juice
1/2 oz. lemon juice
1/2 oz. raspberry syrup
lemon twist and maraschino cherry for garnish

Shake all ingredients in a cocktail shaker with cracked ice. Strain into a chilled cocktail glass. Garnish with a lemon twist and a maraschino cherry.

PLANTATION

This is less sweet than Planter's Punch, *page 22, and simpler to mix. It is another variation on the classic southern rum drink recipe.*

2 oz. dark rum
1 oz. lemon juice
1 dash orange juice
lemon squeeze for garnish

Shake all ingredients in a cocktail shaker with cracked ice. Strain into a chilled cocktail glass. Garnish with a lemon squeeze.

PLANTERS PUNCH

This is not really a punch, but is a famous summer drink. Remember to use your cocktail ratios when mixing this drink: 1 for sour (lemon juice); 2 for sweet (simple syrup); 3 for strong (rum); 4 for weak (orange juice and ice). Sounds like a magic potion!

3 oz. dark rum
1 oz. lemon or lime juice
$\frac{1}{2}$ oz. orange juice, or to taste
2 oz. *Simple Syrup,* page 8
lemon twist for garnish

Shake all ingredients in a cocktail shaker with cracked ice. Strain into a large wine glass filled with ice. Garnish with a lemon twist.

PRESIDENTE

This drink's name refers to the President of Cuba in the late 1920s and early 1930s, Gerardo Machado. He was undone by the effects of the great depression, overthrown in 1933, and succeeded by a succession of short-lived civilian presidents influenced by General Batista, who soon became Cuba's leader.

1½ oz. dark rum
½ oz. dry vermouth
½ oz. Cointreau
½ oz. lemon juice
1 dash grenadine

Shake all ingredients in a cocktail shaker with cracked ice. Strain into a chilled cocktail glass. Garnish with a lemon twist.

FISH HOUSE PUNCH

Here's a party-sized recipe for a punch which is very suitable for a get-together on a chilly evening.

36 oz. dark rum
24 oz. lemon juice, or 30 oz. lime juice
24 oz. brandy
4 oz. peach brandy
¾ lb. superfine sugar
40 oz. water

Dissolve sugar in a small amount of hot water. Add juice and remaining water. 2 hours before serving, add spirits and refrigerate. To serve, pour into a punch bowl and add ice moulds.

SOUTH SEA

Brown rum is different from dark rum: it is aged in oak barrels for six years and is in many ways comparable to brandy, bourbon or whiskey. Dark rum is aged briefly and colored.

2 oz. brown rum
3/4 oz. curaçao
3/4 oz. lime juice

Shake all ingredients in a cocktail shaker with cracked ice. Strain into a chilled cocktail glass. Garnish with a lime squeeze.

PALMETTO

Maraschino cherries are cherries which have been soaked in a sugar syrup, flavored and dyed. Red maraschino cherries are usually almond-flavored, while green maraschinos are mint-flavored.

1 oz. brown rum
1/2 oz. Cointreau
1/2 oz. apricot brandy
1 oz. lemon juice
lemon twist and maraschino cherry for garnish

Shake all ingredients in a cocktail shaker with cracked ice. Strain into a chilled cocktail glass. Garnish with a lemon twist and a maraschino cherry.

PARDO BAR

Amer Picon is a bitter orange-flavored cordial which also contains the medicinal compound gentian. If it is not available, a good substitute is Torani Amer, made by the makers of the Italian syrups used in flavored soft drinks.

2 oz. brown rum
½ oz. Amer Picon
1 dash pernod

Shake all ingredients in a cocktail shaker with cracked ice. Strain into a chilled cocktail glass. Garnish with a lemon twist.

ARAK

Arak is a city in central Iran, famous for its Persian rugs. Enjoy one of these cocktails on the rug, in front of the fire.

1½ oz. dark rum
1½ oz. sherry
1 dash angostura bitters

Shake all ingredients in a cocktail shaker with cracked ice. Strain into a chilled cocktail glass. Garnish with a lemon twist.

DAIQUIRI

President John F. Kennedy was the most famous daiquiri drinker of all. The Kennedy Galleries in St. Petersburg, Florida have an exhibit from the 1962 Presidential campaign with a handwritten note which shows his preference for double daiquiris.

1¹/₂ oz. light rum
¹/₂ oz. lemon juice, or ³/₄ oz. lime juice
¹/₄ oz. *Simple Syrup,* page 8

Shake all ingredients in a cocktail shaker with cracked ice. Strain into a chilled cocktail glass. Garnish with a lime wheel.

HAVANA SIDECAR

The conventional Sidecar cocktail contains brandy, lemon juice and Cointreau: the Havana version simply substitutes rum for brandy.

1½ oz. brown or dark rum
¾ oz. Cointreau
¾ oz. lemon juice
lemon twist for garnish

Shake all ingredients in a cocktail shaker with cracked ice. Strain into a chilled cocktail glass. Garnish with a lemon twist.

BACARDI COCKTAIL

This is very similar to a daiquiri, but sweetened with grenadine rather than simple syrup. The Bacardi Cocktail was in the news in the nineteen thirties. The Bacardi family protested at bars making the bacardi cocktail with other brands of rum, and were successful in court.

3 oz. Bacardi light rum
1 oz. lime juice
½ oz. *Simple Syrup,* page 8
¼ oz. grenadine
lime wheel for garnish

Shake all ingredients in a cocktail shaker with cracked ice. Strain into a chilled martini glass. Garnish with a lime wheel

BACARDI HIGHBALL

Bacardi is practically a synonym for Cuba and gives a romantic/Caribbean flavor to any cocktail. This easy-to-mix drink is very refreshing on a hot afternoon.

2 oz. Bacardi light rum
2 oz. soda water, or to taste
lemon slice for garnish

Stir rum and soda water gently with ice. Strain into a collins or highball glass. Add ice cubes and top with soda. Garnish with a lemon slice.

BAY BREEZE

This drink is similar to the more common, vodka-based Sea Breeze. The name suggests the drink: cool, light, refreshing.

2 oz. light rum
1 dash pineapple juice
cranberry juice to taste
pineapple wedge for garnish

Into an ice-filled highball glass, add rum and pineapple juice. Top up with cranberry juice and stir. Garnish with an umbrella and a pineapple wedge.

BEACHCOMBER

This is another popular cocktail for which there are many variations. Almost all include rum, lime juice and cherry liqueur.

1½ oz. light rum
½ oz. Cointreau
¾ oz. lime juice
2 dashes cherry liqueur
lime wedge for garnish

In a blender container, flash blend ingredients with shaved ice. Pour unstrained mixture into a wine glass. Garnish with a lime wedge.

BEE'S KISS

This cocktail has an unexpected sting, as the cream and honey mask the alcohol in the drink.

1½ oz. light rum
½ oz. dark rum
¾ oz. cream
½–1 tsp. honey

Shake all ingredients in a cocktail shaker over cracked ice. Strain into a chilled cocktail glass. Dust with nutmeg.

CORAL

There are very few places in the world with the right combination of shallow water and warm temperatures to allow the growth of coral reefs offshore. Where you do find coral, you will most certainly also find tropical cocktails like this one.

1½ oz. light rum
¼ oz. apricot brandy
½ oz. lemon juice
¼ oz. grapefruit juice
lemon twist for garnish

Shake all ingredients in a cocktail shaker over cracked ice. Strain into a chilled cocktail glass. Garnish with a lemon twist.

CUBA LIBRE #1

Commonly known as a "rum-and-coke", this is the most familiar and simplest form of the Cuba Libre.

1¼ oz. light rum
4 oz. cola
lime wheel for garnish

Pour rum and cola over ice into a chilled collins glass. Garnish with a lime squeeze.

CUBA LIBRE #2

This version of the Cuba Libre is more complex and flavorful than the simple rum-and-coke version. Gin and rum are often a good combination in cocktails.

1 oz. light rum
$\frac{1}{2}$ oz. gin
$\frac{1}{4}$ oz. lemon juice
3 oz. cola
2 dashes angostura bitters

Pour all ingredients over ice into a chilled collins glass. Garnish with a lime squeeze.

BACARDI PEACH

This drink is a bit more potent in flavor and effect than a regular highball.

1½ oz. Bacardi light rum
1 oz. peach brandy
½ oz. lemon juice
½ oz. *Simple Syrup,* page 8
frosted mint sprig for garnish

Shake all ingredients in a cocktail shaker with cracked ice. Strain into a chilled cocktail glass. Garnish with frosted mint.

CUBA PRESIDENTE

Cointreau is one of several orange liqueurs which are classified as triple sec (triple distilled). Cointreau and Grand Marnier are the best and most expensive of these: they are less sweet than other triple secs. Cointreau is always preferable if it available, but generic triple sec can be substituted when necessary. Curaçao is also a triple sec.

2 oz. light rum
1/2 oz. dry vermouth
1/4 oz. Cointreau
1 dash grenadine
maraschino cherry and lemon twist for garnish

Shake all ingredients in a cocktail shaker with cracked ice. Strain into a chilled cocktail glass. Garnish with maraschino cherry and lemon twist.

DEL MONTE

This is a very old cocktail name, but has no apparent connection with the huge fruit and foods company from California.

1½ oz. light rum
¾ oz. lemon juice
¼ oz. grenadine
maraschino cherry for garnish

Shake all ingredients in a cocktail shaker with cracked ice. Strain into a chilled cocktail glass. Garnish with a maraschino cherry.

FIG LEAF

As cocktails have become increasingly associated with young singles, drink recipe names have become more and more risque: many names are so explicit you'd need a few drinks to say one out loud to a bartender. The name 'fig leaf' comes from an earlier generation of gentler suggestiveness. The modern equivalent, signifying the least you can wear without being naked, might be 'g-string.'

1½ oz. light rum
1 oz. dry vermouth
½ oz. lemon juice
1 dash angostura bitters
lime twist for garnish

Shake all ingredients in a cocktail shaker with cracked ice. Strain into a chilled cocktail glass. Garnish with a lime twist.

FLORIDA DAIQUIRI

This might be considered the older brother of the classic daiquiri: it is a little stronger and sharper in taste than the more traditional drink.

2 oz. light rum
³/₄ oz. curaçao
¹/₂ oz. orange juice
¹/₂ oz. lemon juice
orange slice for garnish

Shake all ingredients in a cocktail shaker with cracked ice. Strain into a chilled cocktail glass. Garnish with an orange slice.

FLORIDITA

The Floridita was a nightclub in Havana made famous by Ernest Hemingway and called the "cradle of the daiquiri." Hemingway was supposed to have had his own extra-large glass at the bar. Note that white crème de cacao has a similar flavor to brown crème de cacao but is white or clear in color.

2 oz. light rum
½ oz. lemon juice, or ¾ oz. lime juice
½ oz. sweet vermouth
1 dash white crème de cacao
1 dash grenadine

Shake all ingredients in a cocktail shaker with cracked ice. Strain into a chilled cocktail glass. Garnish with a lime wheel.

FOX TROT

Slow or quick, the old-time fox trot is a very pleasant dance rhythm and as mellow and gracious as its liquid namesake.

2 oz. light rum
$\frac{1}{4}$ oz. Cointreau
$\frac{1}{2}$ oz. lemon juice
lime wheel for garnish

Shake all ingredients in a cocktail shaker with cracked ice. Strain into a chilled cocktail glass. Garnish with a lime wheel.

HAVANA BEACH

This drink's name conjures up visions of lovers strolling on the beautiful beaches at Varadero or El Salado, but a shady little plaza wherever you are on a sunny evening will do just fine!

1½ oz. light rum
1 oz. pineapple juice
½ oz. lemon juice
¼ oz. *Simple Syrup,* page 8
soda water
pineapple wheel for garnish

Shake all ingredients in a cocktail shaker with cracked ice. Strain into a chilled cocktail glass. Garnish with a pineapple wheel.

LEAVE IT TO ME

Maraschino liqueur is made from marasca cherries. The cherry pits are crushed and included, giving the liqueur a slightly bitter almond-like flavor. This liqueur is not interchangeable with other cherry liqueurs (or maraschino cherries), which are generally much sweeter.

1½ oz. light rum
½ oz. maraschino liqueur
¾ oz. lime juice
¼ oz. raspberry syrup
lime wheel for garnish

Shake all ingredients in a cocktail shaker with cracked ice. Strain into a chilled cocktail glass. Garnish with a lime wheel.

HAVANA CLUB RICKEY

This is another classic rum drink, based simply on rum and lime juice. Vary the amounts of rum and lime juice according to your taste.

1½ oz. light rum
½ oz. fresh lime juice, peel reserved
soda water to taste
mint sprig or lime wheel for garnish
1 dash *Simple Syrup,* page 8, if desired

Squeeze lime into a chilled Old Fashioned glass. Add a piece of lime peel. Top up with soda water. Garnish with a sprig of mint or lime wheel. For a sweeter drink add a little simple syrup with the lime juice.

PEDRO COLLINS

A Tom Collins is a classic cocktail made mainly from gin, lemon juice, a sweetener and soda water. A John Collins is the same drink made with whiskey. A Pedro Collins *is — of course — a similar recipe made with rum.*

2 oz. light rum
1 oz. lemon juice
2 oz. soda water
1 tsp. superfine sugar
maraschino cherry and lime wheel for garnish

Shake rum, juice and sugar in a cocktail shaker with cracked ice. Strain into a chilled collins glass filled with ice. Top up with soda. Garnish with a maraschino cherry and a lime wheel.

HEMINGWAY DAIQUIRI

The great American author Ernest Hemingway is an icon in Cuba. He began visiting in the 1920s, while living in Key West. He moved to Havana in 1940 and lived there for 20 years with his third wife, Martha Gellhorn. Hemingway donated his Nobel Prize for Literature to the Cuban people.

1½ oz. light rum
¼ oz. maraschino liqueur
¾ oz. lime juice, or ½ oz. lemon juice
¼ oz. grapefruit juice
lime wheel for garnish

Shake all ingredients in a cocktail shaker with cracked ice. Strain into a chilled cocktail glass. Garnish with a lime wheel.

HURRICANE

This drink is said to have been dreamed up by an Irishman in New Orleans in the '30s. You can drink this in Ireland — if you can find all the ingredients.

1 oz. light rum
1 oz. dark rum
1 oz. lime juice
$\frac{1}{2}$ oz. passion fruit syrup
lime wheel for garnish

Shake all ingredients in a cocktail shaker with cracked ice. Strain into a tall glass filled with ice. Garnish with a lime wheel and an umbrella.

KICK-A-PU

The origin of this rum-punch drink is unknown but this version comes from an Irish engineer in Venezuela and has an "engineer's guarantee" that it will make the party "go-go-go, ah-one, ah-two, ah-three, ah-four."

1 cup *Simple Syrup,* page 8
1 cup lemon juice
3 cups strong rum
4 cups water

Combine all ingredients in a jug and add ice. Quantities may be adjusted to taste. Empty jars may be substituted for cocktail glasses in an emergency!

MIAMI

Cointreau is the finest-tasting orange liqueur, but it is expensive. If it is not available, or you are on a budget, use triple-sec instead.

2 oz. light rum
³/₄ oz. Cointreau
¹/₂ oz. lemon juice
lemon wedge for garnish

Shake all ingredients in a cocktail shaker with cracked ice. Strain into a chilled cocktail glass. Garnish with a lemon wedge.

MILLIONAIRE

Sloes are the fruit of the blackthorn. Sloe gin is a sweet, red-colored, gin-based liqueur flavored with blackthorn plums. It is traditionally made in Ireland and England.

1½ oz. light rum
1 dash sloe gin
½ oz. apricot brandy
½ oz. lemon juice

Shake all ingredients in a cocktail shaker with cracked ice. Strain into a chilled cocktail glass. Garnish with a lemon squeeze.

MOJITO #1

The Mojito has recently become one of the trendiest cocktails, but it's not a new drink. It's a Cuban classic, and a close cousin to the Southern American specialty, the Mint Julep (which is usually made with bourbon).

2½ oz. light rum
1 lime
½ oz. *Simple Syrup,* page 8
8 mint sprigs
soda water

Place syrup, mint and splash of soda water in a chilled 16oz. glass. Muddle mint by pressing leaves against the side of glass with a spoon to release mint oils and flavor. Slice lime and squeeze both halves into mixture. Leave 1 lime hull in the drink. Add rum, stir and fill glass with ice. Top with soda water and garnish with another mint sprig.

MOJITO #2

Crushing the leaves so they release their oils gives the mojito a powerful mint flavor and aroma. The mint and soda water make this a light and refreshing-tasting drink, with a strong kick.

3 fresh mint sprigs
2 tsp. sugar
3 tbs. fresh lemon or lime juice
1½ oz. light rum
club soda, chilled
lemon slice for garnish

In a tall glass, crush mint with a fork or spoon to release flavor. Add sugar and lemon juice and stir thoroughly. Top with ice. Add rum and mix. Top off with club soda or seltzer. Add a lemon slice and remaining mint.

SAN FRANCISCO MOJITO

Perhaps because the mojito has only recently become extremely popular, you won't find many variations on the basic recipe. However, in San Francisco we found a barman who adds fresh ginger to his recipe. It's a wonderful, refreshing and subtle complement to the mint.

3 fresh mint sprigs
2 tsp. sugar
freshly squeezed juice of 1 lime
1 tbs. grated fresh ginger, or to taste
2 oz. light rum
club soda, chilled
lemon slice for garnish

In a tall glass, crush mint with a spoon or fork to release flavor. Add sugar, lime juice and grated ginger and stir thoroughly. Top with ice. Add rum and mix. Top off with club soda or seltzer. Add a lemon slice.

PAULINE

This recipe is another of the many variations on the basic cocktail ingredients of rum, Cointreau and lemon juice.

1½ oz. light rum
½ oz. Cointreau
1 oz. lemon juice
lemon twist for garnish

Shake all ingredients in a cocktail shaker with cracked ice. Strain into a chilled cocktail glass. Garnish with a lemon twist.

DOREEN GRAY

To paraphrase Oscar Wilde, "After a good cocktail, one can forgive anyone — even one's own relatives."

1½ oz. Mandarine Napoleon
1½ oz. golden rum
2 oz. orange juice
2 oz. cranberry juice

Into a shaker ⅔ filled with ice add Mandarine Napoleon, golden rum, orange juice and cranberry juice. Shake and strain into a martini glass.

PERNOD PAULINE

Pernod is an unusual ingredient in rum cocktails. It is a liquor distilled from star anise and aromatic herbs.

1½ oz. light rum
½ oz. Cointreau
1 oz. lemon juice
1 dash Pernod
lemon twist for garnish

Shake all ingredients in a cocktail shaker with cracked ice. Strain into a chilled cocktail glass. Garnish with a lemon twist.

SANTIAGO JULEP

Grenadine is a deep, red, sweet syrup made from pomegranates. It is usually made as a non-alcoholic cordial, but may also be found as a liqueur.

2 oz. light rum
1 oz. lime juice
1 oz. pineapple juice
$\frac{1}{2}$ oz. grenadine
6 mint sprigs
mint sprig for garnish

Place mint and grenadine in a pint glass. Muddle mint by pressing leaves against the side of glass with a spoon to release mint oils and flavor. Add lime, pineapple juice and rum. Pack with shaved ice. Garnish with a mint sprig.

RANGER

Here's another cocktail combining the smoothness and kick of gin and rum.

1 oz. light rum
1 oz. gin
$\frac{1}{2}$ oz. lemon juice
1 dash *Simple Syrup,* page 8

Shake all ingredients in a cocktail shaker with cracked ice. Strain into a chilled cocktail glass. Garnish with a lemon twist.

RILEY

Mt. Gay Eclipse rum is from the oldest distillery in Barbados, dating to 1809. It is an excellent, amber-colored, medium-bodied rum and should be available at specialty liquor stores or via the internet. Any light rum will work in this drink if Mt. Gay is not available.

1 oz. Mt. Gay Eclipse rum, or
    other light rum
½ oz. Cointreau
½ oz. lemon juice
½ oz. orange juice

½ oz. lime juice
1 dash crème de cassis
1 dash raspberry syrup
lime squeeze for garnish

Shake all ingredients except raspberry syrup in a cocktail shaker with cracked ice. Strain into a chilled cocktail glass and add raspberry syrup. Garnish with a lime squeeze.

XYZ

This is a distinctive cocktail because it has unusual proportions of rum and Cointreau.

½ oz. light rum
¾ oz. Cointreau
¾ oz. lemon juice
lemon twist for garnish

Shake all ingredients in a cocktail shaker with cracked ice. Strain into a chilled cocktail glass. Garnish with a lemon twist.

RUM JULEP

This drink is very similar to a mojito and the more well-known, whiskey-based Mint Julep.

3 oz. light rum
1/2 oz. *Simple Syrup,* page 8
5 mint sprigs
mint sprig and lemon slice for garnish

Place ingredients in a pint glass with cubed ice. Muddle mint by pressing leaves against the side of glass with a spoon to release mint oils and flavor. Strain ingredients into a serving glass filled with shaved ice. Garnish with mint sprig and a slice of lemon.

SOUTHERN CROSS

This drink crosses equal parts rum and brandy: hence the name.

1 oz. light rum
1 oz. brandy
½ oz. lime juice
¼ oz. *Simple Syrup,* page 8
lime squeeze for garnish

Shake all ingredients in a cocktail shaker with cracked ice. Strain into a chilled cocktail glass. Garnish with a lime squeeze.

SUNSHINE

Crème de cassis is a liqueur made from black currants, often mixed with white wine and served as 'kir'. If crème de cassis is not available, black-currant syrup works well.

1 oz. light rum
1 oz. dry vermouth
½ oz. crème de cassis
½ oz. lemon juice
lemon twist for garnish

Shake all ingredients in a cocktail shaker with cracked ice. Strain into a chilled cocktail glass. Garnish with a lemon twist.

TROPICAL

This is a another, simpler variation on the Daiquiri, *page 29, or the* Florida Daiquiri, *page 43.*

1½ oz. light rum
¾ oz. curaçao
¾ oz. lime juice
lime squeeze for garnish

Shake all ingredients in a cocktail shaker with cracked ice. Strain into a chilled cocktail glass. Garnish with a lime squeeze.

PINA COLADA #1

The Pina Colada is both one of the most famous rum cocktails, and one of the most famous blended drinks. It is synonymous with tropical weather, good times, coconuts and pineapples — all of which are ingredients.

3 oz. light rum
3 tbs. coconut milk
3 tbs. pineapple, chopped

Place all ingredients in a blender container with 2 cups crushed ice. Blend at a high speed for 10 to 15 seconds or until mixture is fairly smooth. Strain into a collins glass and serve with a straw.

PINA COLADA #2

Like all blended cocktails, the Pina Colada is considered a bit kitschy by some, but the basic ingredients of rum, pineapple and coconut milk are hard to beat. This version adds cream for extra smoothness.

3 oz. golden rum
1 oz. coconut milk
$\frac{1}{2}$ oz. cream
$\frac{1}{2}$ oz. pineapple juice
pineapple slice for garnish

In a blender container, mix rum, coconut milk, cream, pineapple juice and ice. Blend and pour into a hurricane glass. Garnish with a slice of pineapple.

HOT BUTTERED RUM

This is a classic winter drink: warming and soothing.

3 oz. dark rum
1 tbs. *Simple Syrup,* page 8
3 cloves
1 cinnamon stick
boiling water
2 tsp. unsalted butter
grated nutmeg for garnish

Into an Irish coffee glass (or anything similar, as long as it can with-stand heat) add dark rum and simple syrup. Add cloves and cinnamon stick and top up with boiling water. Add unsalted butter and grated nutmeg on top.

RUM TODDY

This may not cure your cold, but it will certainly make you feel better.

2 oz. dark rum
2 oz. boiling water
½ tsp. honey
1 dash lemon, or more to taste
cloves to taste

Stir the honey into the rum. Pour boiling water over spoon to dissolve remaining honey. Stir, add lemon and cloves. Serve in bed or on the sofa with a blanket.

ZOMBIE

You can layer the liquid ingredients of a cocktail if they are of different densities. Sugary, sweet liquids are very dense and go to the bottom unless stirred. The higher the proof of the alcohol (like Demerara rum) the less dense it will be and the easier to 'float' on top of the drink.

1½ oz. brown rum
¾ oz. Jamaica dark rum
¾ oz. light rum
¾ oz. pineapple juice
¾ oz. papaya juice

1 oz. lime juice
¼ oz. *Simple Syrup,* page 8
½ oz. 151-proof Demerara rum
    for floating
pineapple wheel for garnish

Shake all ingredients except Demerara rum in a cocktail shaker with cracked ice. Strain into a chilled hurricane glass. Hold a spoon upside down at the surface of the drink. Float Demerara rum on top of the drink by pouring very slowly over the back of the spoon. Garnish with a pineapple wheel and a cherry.

CHOCOLATE COCKTAIL

Remember that liquors with high alcohol content are less dense and will, if poured carefully, float on top of other liquids in a layered drink. Demerara rum or other high-proof rums work well for floating or igniting on top of cocktails.

1 oz. white rum
1 oz. dark rum
1 oz. crème de menthe
1 oz. single cream
1 egg white
1/2 oz. dark or Demerara rum for floating

Into a shaker 2/3 filled with ice, add white rum, dark rum, crème de menthe and single cream. Add egg white, shake and strain into an ice-filled highball. Float a layer of dark rum on top and sprinkle with cocoa powder.

INDEX